Content

SHALOM!

BIBLE TIMES MUSICAL INSTRUMENTS

BIBLE TIMES BASKETS & MATS

PROJECTS WITH PAPER

BIBLE TIMES WRITING

Shalom!

STEP BACK INTO BIBLE TIMES!

Hoop earrings

Tambourine

Make Bible times music with handmade lyres, flutes, tambourines and sistrums.

Lyre

Scroll

Clay tablet

Through all these activities learn about the people of Bible times and their faith in God.

Crafts with a message

A note for parents and teachers

■ Every project in *Bible Crafts 2* includes a linked Bible verse.

■ Many have drawings showing how that item was used in Bible times.

■ You may want to provide photocopies of verses and/or drawings

for children to attach to their crafts. Here are some examples of ways to use verses and drawings to enhance the craft projects in this book.

Getting Ready

If you're planning to do crafts with a child at home, here are some helpful tips:

■ Focus on the crafts suitable for your child's age – but don't ignore projects for older or younger children. Older children enjoy many of the projects for preschool and nursery children. And younger children are always interested in doing "big school" things. Just plan on working with the child, helping with tasks the child can't handle alone.

■ Start with projects which use materials you already have around the house. Make a list of things you don't have that are needed for projects you think your child will enjoy.

■ If materials are difficult to obtain, you can usually come up with alternatives. And often the home-made version ends up being better the original.

If you're planning to lead a group of children doing craft projects, keep these hints in mind:

■ Choose projects that let the children work with a variety of materials.

■ Choose which projects to do far enough in advance to allow time to gather all needed supplies. Many projects use some of the same things.

■ Make up a sample of each project to be sure you understand the directions and can avoid possible problems. You may want to alter some projects to simplify them, or change the materials used.

■ Many materials can be obtained as gifts from people or businesses if you plan ahead and make your needs known. Some materials can be brought by the children themselves. Most can be found in craft shops.

In this book you will find lots of things to do and make. Before you start, you need the right materials and tools. Start collecting them in boxes. Here are some ideas:

Paper box
White card
Tissue paper
Cardboard tubes
Newspaper
Thick card
Corrugated card
Small boxes
Matchboxes

Glue and paintbox
Poster paints
String
PVA glue
Felt-tip pens
Glitter tubes
Sticky tape
Glue stick
Paper clips
Rubber bands

Fabric box
Wool
Cotton
Odd bits of cloth
Scraps of patterned fabric
Elastic

Tool box
Scissors
Craft knife
Ruler
Tape measure
Pencil
Paintbrushes

Bible Times

Musical Instruments

Cymbals

15 Minutes

Ages 3 – 5

Materials
- Felt
- Ruler
- Scissors
- Permanent felt-tip pens

For each child
- Two 22.5cm (9 inch) tinfoil pie pans
- 4 paper fasteners

Preparation by grown-up
- Cut felt into 5 x 12.5cm (2 x 5 inch) strips – two for each child.

Method
- Use felt-tips to decorate your cymbals (*sketch a*).
- Use paper fasteners to fix felt handles to the backs of the cymbals (*sketch b*).
- Hold cymbals by handles and clash them together to play (*sketch c*).

Life in Bible Times
Cymbals are rhythm instruments made of metal. Hitting the metal pieces together makes a very loud sound.

In Bible times, cymbals were played when people praised God at the Temple. Cymbals were played at the beginning or ending of a song or when people weren't singing. Why do you think cymbals weren't played while people were singing?

David and the whole house of Israel were celebrating with all their might before the Lord, with songs and with harps, lyres, tambourines, sistrums and cymbals.
2 Samuel 6:5

a.

b.

felt strip

paper fastener

c.

Trumpet

Materials

■ Garden hose
■ Heavy-duty shears or knife
■ Scissors
■ Masking tape
■ Ruler
■ Aluminium (aluminum) foil
■ Permanent felt-tip pens
For each child
■ 1 plastic funnel

Preparation by grown-up

■ Cut hose into 25cm (10 inch) lengths – one for each child.
■ Cut foil into 50cm (20 inch) lengths – one for each child.

Method

■ Place hose length over thin end of funnel (*sketch a*).
■ Wrap masking tape around end of hose and end of funnel to fix them together (*sketch b*).
■ Use felt-tips to decorate the shiny side of foil.
■ Wrap funnel and hose with aluminium (aluminum) foil, shiny side out.
■ To play, blow into pipe and make a trumpet sound.

Life in Bible Times

In Bible times, trumpets were made of silver or bronze. They were played to make announcements on special days. A trumpet might be played to tell people it was time to come to a big party or to tell soldiers it was time to start a battle.

The Bible tells us that when Jesus returns, we will hear a loud trumpet sound. What would you like to announce with your trumpet?

"They will see the Son of Man coming on the clouds of the sky, with power and great glory. And he will send his angels with a loud trumpet call…"
Matthew 24:30–31

a.

funnel

hose

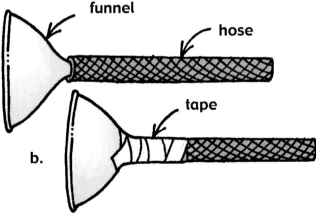

tape

b.

doot da doo

Tambourine

15 Minutes

Ages 4 – 7

Materials

■ Crêpe-paper streamers
■ Scissors
■ Ruler
■ Hole punches
■ Chenille wires (pipe cleaners)
■ Transparent tape

For each child
■ 1 sturdy paper plate
■ 4 jingle bells

Preparation

■ Cut chenille wires (pipe cleaners) into 10cm (4 inch) lengths – four for each child.

■ Cut crêpe paper into 30cm (12 inch) lengths – two for each child.

Method

■ Use hole punch to punch four holes around edge of paper plate (*see sketch*).

■ Thread a chenille wire piece through one of the holes.

■ Thread a bell onto chenille wire.

■ Twist ends of wire together to fasten.

■ Repeat previous three steps to add three more bells to tambourine.

■ Tape streamers to edge of tambourine.

■ Tap finger in middle or shake

Life in Bible Times

In Bible times, tambourines were played when people got together to celebrate or worship. In a book of the Bible called Psalms, the writer tells people to get out their musical instruments and worship God with music and dancing! What song will you sing to God as you play your tambourine?

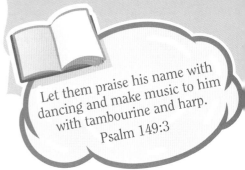

Let them praise his name with dancing and make music to him with tambourine and harp.

Psalm 149:3

Sistrum

15 Minutes

Ages 6 – 9

Materials
- Wire cutter
- Pliers
- Fine gauge wire
- Ruler
- Crêpe-paper streamers
- Scissors
- PVA glue
- Transparent tape

For each child
- 1 wire coat hanger
- 8 buttons/beads

Preparation by grown-up
- Bend the hooked end of each hanger into a long closed loop (*sketch a*).
- Cut off bottom section of wire on hanger (*sketch b*).
- Bend remaining wires to form a wishbone shape (*sketch c*).

- Use pliers to twist the ends of wire into small closed loops (*sketch d*).
- Cut fine gauge wire into 30cm (12 inch) lengths – one for each child.
- Cut crêpe paper into 60cm (24 inch) lengths – one for each child.

Method
- Twist one end of wire length around one of the small loops on hanger (*sketch e*).
- Thread buttons onto wire.
- Twist loose end of wire around second loop on hanger, making it as tight as possible.
- Wind crêpe paper up and down around the base of hanger to cover handle. Before winding paper for the last time, squeeze a line of glue down the middle to secure paper in place (*sketch f*).
- Press end of paper in place. Tape end of paper to secure.
- To play, shake sistrum to make a rattling sound.

Life in Bible Times
Can you name some percussion instruments? (Drums, tambourine, cymbals, triangle, timpani, blocks, bongos.) The sistrum was an Egyptian percussion instrument used in Bible times. It was made of metal and usually had an oval loop with cross-pieces. The cross-pieces held loose rings that jangled together when the sistrum was shaken.

David and the whole house of Israel were celebrating with all their might before the Lord, with songs and with harps, lyres, tambourines, sistrums and cymbals.

2 Samuel 6:5

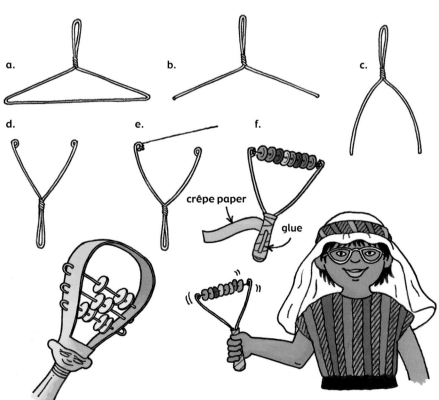

a.   b.   c.

d.   e.   f.

crêpe paper

glue

Lyre

Materials

- Woodgrain effect adhesive material (Fablon) – from DIY (hardware) store
- Ruler
- Scissors
- Transparent tape

For each child

- 1 tissue box
- 2 pencil-sized twigs or dowel rods
- 5 large rubber bands of different widths

Preparation by grown-up

- Measure and cut adhesive material to cover each tissue box.

Method

- Remove backing and wrap self-adhesive paper around tissue box. Make sure seam is on bottom of box.
- Fold ends as if you were wrapping a package and tape to secure (sketch a).
- Cut slashes in adhesive paper where it covers opening in box (sketch b). Fold back cut paper to reveal opening (sketch c).
- Stretch rubber bands lengthways around box.
- Carefully put a twig underneath rubber bands on each end of box (sketch d).
- Pluck and strum rubber bands to play lyre.

Life in Bible Times

What instrument do you know how to play? What instrument would you like to learn? Many people in Bible times played small harps called lyres. Lyres were stringed instruments with wooden frames.

One boy who played a lyre was a shepherd named David. He probably took his lyre when caring for his sheep. King Saul asked David to play the lyre for him. The music soothed the king when he was in a bad mood. When you're in a bad mood, what helps you feel better?

I will sing a new song to you, O God; on the ten-stringed lyre I will make music to you…
Psalm 144:9

a.

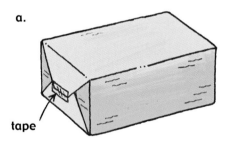

tape

b.

cut

c.

d.

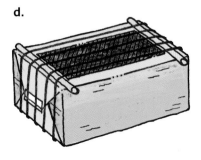

Shepherd's Flute

Materials

- Bamboo (from craft shop)
- Utility knife
- Felt-tip pens
- Rulers
- Hammers
- Nails
- Saw
- Sandpaper

Preparation by grown-up

- Beginning about 1.25cm (½ inch) below plugged joint, saw bamboo into 25 to 30cm (10 to 12 inch) lengths – one for each child. One end of each length should be plugged and one end should be open.

- Use utility knife to whittle a v-shaped notch in open end of each bamboo length (sketch a).

Method

- Use sandpaper to sand rough edges of flute.

- On the notched side of pipe, beginning 2.5cm (1 inch) from plugged end, use felt-tip pen to mark six dots on pipe. Dots should be about 1.25cm (½ inch) apart (sketch b).

- Ask a friend to hold the flute while you hammer a nail into each marked spot. Hammer carefully, just enough to make a small hole (sketch b).

- Cover all six holes with fingers as you hold flute (sketch c).

- Blow into flute so that your breath is split by the notch. It will sound like a whistle. (This may take some practice.)

- Play different notes by blowing into flute and lifting fingers off holes.

Life in Bible Times

In Bible times, every shepherd owned a simple pipe or flute made from two hollowed-out pieces of cane. They would play their flutes to help pass the time while they were out watching their goats or sheep. Also, flutes were played along with other instruments as a way of praising God.

Praise him with tambourine and dancing, praise him with the strings and flute.
Psalm 150:4

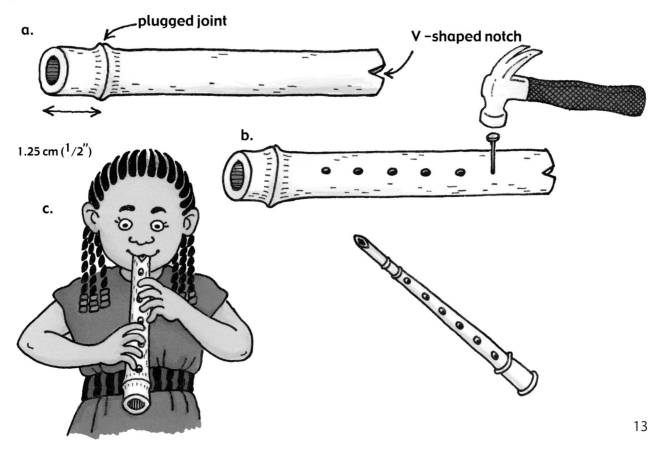

a. plugged joint

V –shaped notch

1.25 cm (¹/2")

b.

c.

Pipes

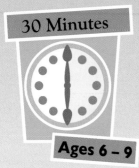
Materials

- Bamboo (from craft shop)
- Saw
- Tape Measure
- String
- Scissors
- Masking tape
- Sandpaper

Optional

- If bamboo is not available, use garden hose. Glue cardboard on the ends to plug them.

Preparation by grown-up

- Use saw to cut five bamboo lengths (each with a plugged joint at one end and open at opposite end), the shortest being 11.25cm (4½ inches) long and each consecutive length being 1.25cm (½ inch) longer – one set for each child.
- Cut string into 135cm (1½ yard) lengths – two for each child.

Method

- Use sandpaper to sand rough edges of bamboo lengths.
- Tear off a 30cm (12 inch) length of tape and lay it on table, sticky side up.
- Position bamboo lengths on tape, side by side, from shortest to longest, with open ends of bamboo in line (sketch a).
- Wrap ends of tape around bamboo. (The tape will hold bamboo in place while you are lacing it together.)
- Beginning at shortest pipe, take one length of string around end of bamboo and tie about 2.5cm (1 inch) from top (sketch b).
- Wrap string around each pipe, tying to secure (sketch c).
- When you reach the last bamboo length, tie string around pipes a second time, working in the opposite direction (sketch d).
- Tie a knot at the end and cut off excess string.
- Repeat process to secure opposite ends of bamboo.
- Remove tape.
- To play, blow across bamboo lengths as you would blow across a bottle top.

Life in Bible Times

Simple flutes, made from hollowed out pieces of cane, were commonly used in Bible times. Sometimes several cane pieces were laced together to make an instrument called "pipes". When blown into, each pipe made a different sound according to its length.

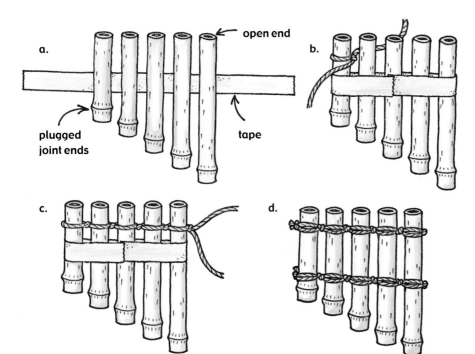

a. plugged joint ends / open end / tape

b.

c.

d.

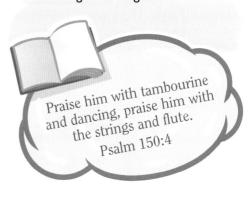

Praise him with tambourine and dancing, praise him with the strings and flute.
Psalm 150:4

Finger Cymbals

15 Minutes

Ages 4 – 6

Materials

For each child

■ 2 large buttons with large holes

■ 2 size 14 rubber bands

■ 1 toothpick

Method

■ Thread a rubber band through two holes in button (*sketch a*).

If necessary, use toothpick to push rubber band through holes.

■ Repeat to make second cymbal.

■ To play, fasten cymbals to your fingers and tap out a rhythm (*sketch b*).

Life in Bible Times

In Bible times, cymbals were a popular instrument used to worship God. They were made of metal and were about the size of dinner plates. When two cymbals were hit together they made a loud crashing sound.

Praise him with the clash of cymbals, praise him with resounding cymbals.
Psalm 150:5

a.

b.

Bible Times

Writing

Ancient Scroll

30 Minutes

Ages 4 – 8

Materials
- Greek and Hebrew alphabets and/ or Hebrew words (*pp. 18-20*)
- Black paint
- Paintbrushes
- Shallow plastic containers
- Wool
- Newspapers
- Scissors
- Ruler
- Photocopier

For each child
- Brown wrapping paper

Preparation by grown-up
- Cut wool into 30cm (12 inch) lengths – one for each child.
- Photocopy pages with Greek and Hebrew alphabets and/or Hebrew words – one for each child.
- Pour paint into containers.
- Cover work area with newspapers.

Method
- Cut paper to right size (*sketch a*).
- Crumple sheet (*sketch b*) and smooth out. Repeat crumpling process several times. (This will give the sheet an ancient look.)
- Use paint to copy Hebrew or Greek letters onto crumpled sheet (*sketch c*).
- Allow to dry.
- Roll up sheet and tie with wool (*sketch d*).

For younger children
Use felt-tip pens to copy a short Bible verse or the word *Shalom* on scrolls. Teacher cuts rectangle for younger children. Younger children use felt-tips to draw a picture on scrolls.

Life in Bible Times
What is our paper made from? (Trees.) In Bible times, paper was made from the stems of a plant called papyrus. Papyrus strips were beaten together into long sheets and rolled to make scrolls. Other scrolls were made from parchment – goat or sheep skins that had been dried and stretched.

[Jesus] went to Nazareth ... and on the Sabbath day he went into the synagogue ... And he stood up to read. The scroll of the prophet Isaiah was handed to him.

Luke 4:16–17

a.

b.

c.

d.

HEBREW ALPHABET

(WITH PHONETIC VALUES)

Note: The Hebrew alphabet reads from right to left. Also, several Hebrew characters are not included here because they have no English equivalent.

d	g	b	a
ד	ג	ב	א
dalet (*DOLL-ed*)	gimmal (*Gee-mel*)	bet (*bait*)	alef (*AH-lif*)

h	z	v, w, o, u	ă, h
ח	ז	ו	ה
chet (*khet*)	zayin (*ZI-on*)	vav (*vov*)	heh (*hay*)

m	l	k	ē, ĭ, y
מ	ל	כ	י
mem (*mem*)	lamed (*LA-med*)	kaf (*khaf*)	yod (*yode*)

p	p, f	s	n
ק	פ	ס	נ
qof (*qofe*)	pe (*pay*)	samekh (*SAM-ekh*)	nun (*noon*)

t	sh	r
ת	ש	ר
tav (*tav*)	shin (*sheen*)	resh (*resh*)

GREEK ALPHABET

GREEK		ROMAN	GREEK		ROMAN
alpha	A	A	kappa	K	K
bēta	B	B	lambda	L	L
gamma	Γ	G	mu	M	M
delta	△	D	nu	N	N
epsilon	E	E	xi	Ξ	KSI
(digamma) upsilon	Y	FY	omicron	O	O
zēta	Z	Z	pi	Γ	P
ēta	H	H	rhō	P	R
thēta	⊙	TH	sigma	Ϲ	S
iota	I	I	tau	T	T

BE A BIBLE TIMES SCRIBE

Copy Hebrew words onto a scroll or tablet.
(Hebrew is written from right to left!)

Shalom (peace)

שָׁלוֹם

Psalm 33:11
"The plans of the Lord stand firm forever."

עֲצַת יהוה לְעוֹלָם תַעֲמֹד

Psalm 100:3
"It is he who made us,

הוּא עָשָׂנוּ

and we are his."

וְלוֹ אֲנַחְנוּ

Scribes copied the words of the Bible onto scrolls letter by letter.
Imagine how long it took to make a copy of all 66 books of the Bible!

Clay Tablet & Writing Stick

Ages 4 – 9

Materials

- Air-drying clay
- Rolling pin
- Utility knife
- Table knives

For each child
- 1 craft stick

Preparation by grown-up

- Divide clay into fist-sized balls.
- Use utility knife to sharpen one end of each craft stick.

Method

DAY ONE
- Flatten ball of clay with your hand.
- Use rolling pin to flatten clay into a slab about 1.25cm (½ inch) thick.
- Use table knife to cut slab into a square or rectangular shape.
- Use sharpened craft stick to scratch initials onto bottom of tablet.
- Allow to dry.

DAY TWO
- After tablet is dry, use sharpened craft stick to scratch letters onto tablet.

Life in Bible Times

If you want to leave a message for someone, what do you do? In Bible times, people wrote messages and bills on broken pieces of pottery.

God told Isaiah to write an important message on a tablet. Isaiah may have written God's message on clay tablets made from broken pottery.

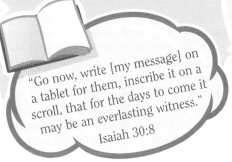

"Go now, write [my message] on a tablet for them, inscribe it on a scroll, that for the days to come it may be an everlasting witness."
Isaiah 30:8

sharpened craft stick

Pyhlactery

45 Minutes

Ages 6 – 9

Materials
- Bibles
- Light brown bias binding (tape)
- Brown wrapping paper
- Scissors
- Ruler
- White PVA glue diluted with water
- Shallow plastic containers
- White paper
- Fine felt-tip pens
- Embroidery thread or wool

For each child
- Small cardboard gift box available from craft shops

Preparation by grown-up
- Cut bias binding into 75cm (30 inch) lengths – one for each child.
- Cut white paper into 5 x 7.5cm (2 x 3 inch) pieces – two for each child.
- Cut thread or wool into 20cm (8 inch) lengths – two for each child.

Method
DAY ONE
- Tear brown paper into small pieces about 2.5 x 5cm (1 x 2 inches).
- Soak paper pieces in diluted glue.
- Smooth soaked paper pieces onto outside of box and lid to cover completely (*sketch a*). Let dry.

DAY TWO
- Position length of bias binding in middle bottom of box and glue (*sketch b*). Let dry.
- Look up one or two verses in the Bible and copy them onto small pieces of paper. (Teacher or parent may want to suggest a verse.)
- Roll up paper and tie with thread or wool (*sketch c*). Place inside box.
- Tie phylactery to your forehead.

Life in Bible Times
A phylactery is a little leather box containing God's commandments written on rolls of parchment. In Bible times, Jewish men wore phylacteries on their arms and foreheads to remind them of God's words. What helps you remember God's words?

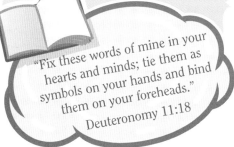

"Fix these words of mine in your hearts and minds; tie them as symbols on your hands and bind them on your foreheads."
Deuteronomy 11:18

a.
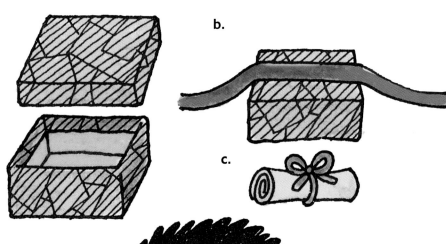

b.

c.

Scribe's Inkhorn

Two-day project

45 Minutes

Ages 6 – 9

Materials

- Brown wrapping paper or craft paper
- Scissors
- PVA glue
- PVA glue diluted with water
- Masking tape
- Plastic containers
- Cardboard
- Ruler
- String
- Bradawl
- Newspaper

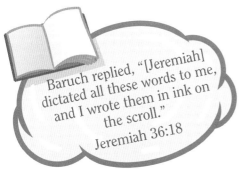

Baruch replied, "[Jeremiah] dictated all these words to me, and I wrote them in ink on the scroll."
Jeremiah 36:18

Life in Bible Times

In Bible times, many people didn't know how to read or write. If a person needed to write a letter, he would go to the local scribe, who sat in the marketplace or another public place. Sometimes a scribe carried a horn filled with ink on his belt. The ink was made of carbon from charcoal, mixed with oil and water. A scribe's "pen" was made from a reed or rush.

Besides writing letters, scribes were also hired to copy the Scriptures. It took a long time to make an entire copy of the Bible. That's why every copy was very precious.

For each child
- 1 cardboard tube

Preparation

- Cut cardboard into 5cm (2 inch) circles – one for each child.
- Cut string into 15cm (6 inch) lengths – one for each child.
- Cut additional string into 10cm (4 inch) lengths – one for each child.
- Cut tubes into 15cm (6 inch) lengths – one for each child.
- Pour diluted glue into plastic containers.
- Cover work area with newspaper.

Method

DAY ONE

- Cut several 5cm (2 inch) slits halfway round bottom of tube (sketch a).
- Press slit side towards unslit side and tape to form a point at end of tube (sketch b).
- Wrinkle brown paper to soften.

Tear into strips about 2.5cm (1 inch) wide.

- Soak strips in diluted glue. Apply strips to tube to cover it completely (sketch c).
- Glue shorter length of string around the edge of the cardboard circle (sketch d).
- Cover both sides of cardboard circle (and string) with brown paper strips.
- Let dry.

DAY TWO

- Teacher use bradawl to poke two holes in lid and two holes in middle of back of inkhorn (sketch e).
- Thread longer length of string through all four holes and tie to attach lid to horn (sketch f). The rim (string) side of cap should face down.
- Tuck inkhorn in your belt.

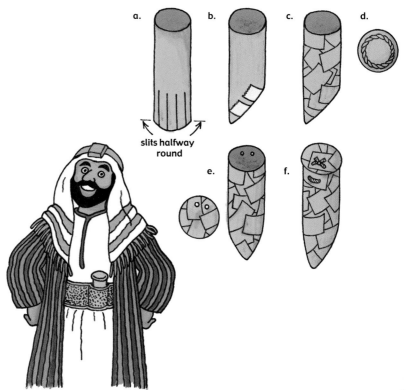

a. b. c. d.

slits halfway round

e. f.

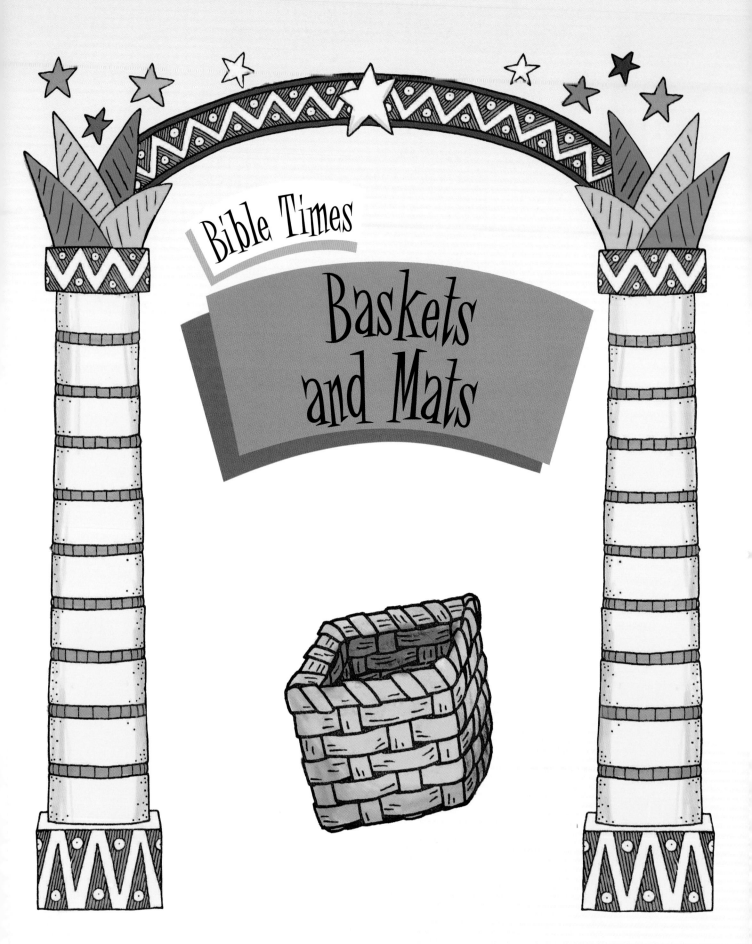

Bible Times

Baskets and Mats

Woven Paper Mat

30 Minutes

Ages 4 – 7

Materials
- Bright paper in 22.5 x 30cm (9 x 12 inch) sheets
- Scissors
- Glue stick or PVA glue
- Pencil
- Ruler

Preparation by grown-up
- Fold sheet of paper in half along shorter side – one for each child.
- Measure and draw slit lines along folded edge at 2.5cm (1 inch) intervals, stopping 2.5cm (1 inch) from edge of paper (*sketch a*).
- Cut contrasting paper into 2.5 x 22.5cm (1 x 9 inch) strips – six for each child.

Method
- Cut along slit lines on folded sheet of paper.
- Unfold paper.
- Weave a strip of paper through slits, over and under, over and under, etc. (*sketch b*).
- Weave a second strip through slits, under and over, under and over, etc.
- Weave remaining strips through slits, alternating pattern with each strip (*sketch c*).
- Glue ends of strips to edges of paper.

Life in Bible Times
What are your clothes made of? In Bible times, clothes were made from sheep's wool. Weavers used wooden looms to weave the wool thread into cloth. How long did it take you to weave your mat? How long do you think it would take to weave small threads into a piece of cloth big enough for a tunic?

For Aaron and his sons, they made tunics of fine linen – the work of a weaver...
Exodus 39:27

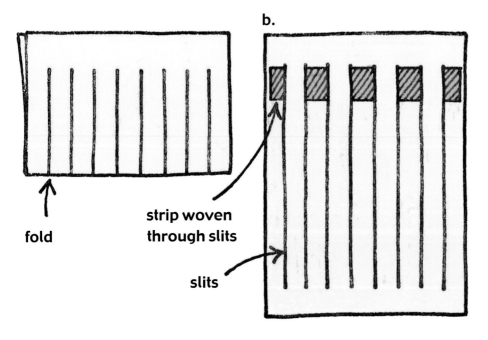

a.

fold

b.

strip woven through slits

slits

c.

Woven Cloth Mat

30 Minutes

Ages 6 – 9

Materials

- Hessian (burlap)
- Assorted wool
- Scissors
- Tape measure
- Drill
- 4mm ($^3/_{16}$ inch) drill bit

For each child

- 1 craft stick

Preparation by grown-up

- Cut hessian into 27.5 x 42.5cm (11 x 17 inch) rectangles – one for each child.

- Cut wool into 37.5cm (15 inch) lengths – about ten for each child.
- Drill a hole in the end of each craft stick.

Method

- Thread one length of wool onto craft stick (*sketch a*).
- Pull out four consecutive threads from anywhere on long edge of hessian to make an opening (*sketch b*).
- Leading with craft stick, weave in and out of threads in this open space (*sketch c*).
- Repeat previous three steps to weave additional strands of wool into hessian (*sketch d*).

For younger children

Teacher or parent pulls threads from hessian beforehand.

Life in Bible Times

In Bible times, most cloth was made from sheep's wool. The wool was cut from the sheep, combed, washed and dyed. Next, the wool was spun on a spindle, twisting the wool into yarn. Then the yarn was woven into cloth on a wooden loom. Many times clothing, blankets and mats were made from a single, uncut piece of cloth.

This garment was seamless, woven in one piece from top to bottom.
John 19:23

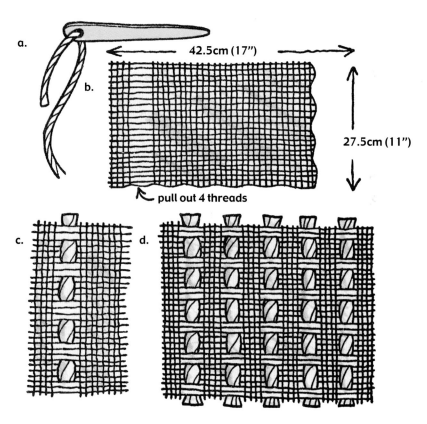

a.

b.

42.5cm (17")

27.5cm (11")

pull out 4 threads

c.

d.

Paper Mat

30 Minutes

Ages 6 – 9

Materials

- Scissors
- Paper or raffia strips
- Ruler
- PVA glue

Preparation

- Cut paper into 28cm (11 inch) lengths – eight for each child.
- Cut additional paper into 35.5cm (14 inch) lengths – 14 for each child.

Method

- Place the eight shorter paper strip lengths in front of you (*sketch a*). Leave a 1.25cm (½ inch) space between each strip.
- Weave a longer paper strip over and under, over and under the eight strips (*sketch a*).
- Next to first woven strip, weave a second strip under and over, under and over the eight lengths.
- Repeat process to add remaining strips, alternating weaving pattern with each strip of paper you add (*sketch b*).
- Glue outside edges of mat together to secure. Let dry.

Life in Bible Times

Where do you like to lie down to rest? In Bible times, people often rested on woven mats made from grasses or reeds. After Jesus healed a lame man, He told the man to get up, take his mat and go home.

He got up, took his mat and walked out in full view of them all. This amazed everyone and they praised God, saying, "We have never seen anything like this!"
Mark 2:12

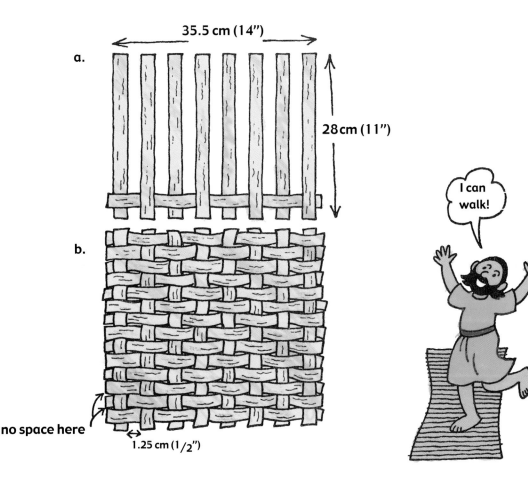

a.

35.5 cm (14")

28cm (11")

b.

no space here

1.25 cm (1/2")

I can walk!

Fish Net

30 Minutes

Ages 8 – 11

Materials

■ Heavy string
■ Scissors
■ Tape measure

Preparation by grown-up

■ Cut string into 1.8m (2 yard) lengths – one for each child.

Method

■ Make a loop with string near one end and tie a knot (*sketch a*). This knotted end will be called the "standing end".

■ Bring other end of string up and through the first loop, forming a second loop below (*sketch b*). Use left-hand thumb and index finger to pinch working end of string between strands of original loop.

■ At point you are pinching with left hand, use right hand to tie a knot with working end (*sketch c*).

■ Pull string tight to secure (*sketch d*).

■ Repeat previous three steps to add the next loop (*sketch e*).

■ Continue adding loops until net is right size (*sketch f*).

Life in Bible Times

Have you ever been fishing? What did you use to catch fish? Jesus' disciples, Peter, Andrew, James and John, were fishermen on the Sea of Galilee. They used nets to catch fish. The nets had weights tied to them. When the fishermen saw fish in the water, they dropped a net into the water. The weights carried the net down, trapping the fish underneath. Then the fishermen pulled the net full of fish through the water to shore.

As Jesus was walking beside the Sea of Galilee, he saw two brothers, Simon called Peter and his brother Andrew. They were casting a net into the lake, for they were fishermen. "Come, follow me," Jesus said, "and I will make you fishers of men." At once they left their nets and followed him.

Matthew 4:18–20

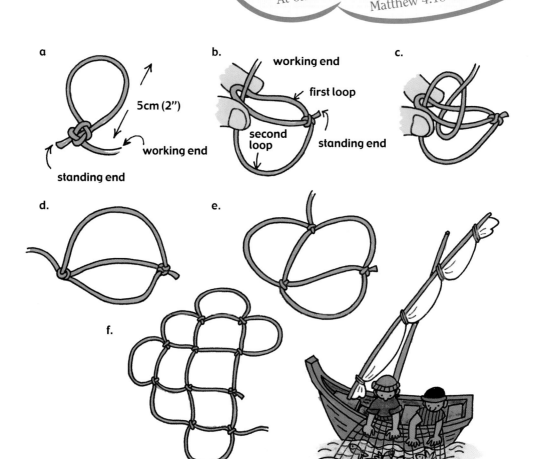

King's Fan

Materials

- Bamboo (from craft shop) or 2.5cm (1 inch) dowel
- Tape measure
- PVA glue
- Transparent tape
- Scissors
- Lightweight cardboard
- String
- Saw

For each child

- Two sheets of 27.5 x 42.5cm (11 x 17 inch) green paper

Preparation by grown-up

- Saw the bamboo or dowel into 90cm (1 yard) lengths – one for each child.

- Cut the string into 90cm (1 yard) lengths – one for each child.
- Cut the cardboard into 2.5 x 15cm (1 x 6 inch) strips – two for each child.

Method

- Tape two sheets of the paper end-to-end (*sketch a*).
- Fold paper into 2.5cm (1 inch) accordion folds (*sketch b*).
- Place glue on half of each cardboard strip and attach a strip to each end of paper (*sketch c*). Let dry.
- Lay top 7.5cm (3 inches) of bamboo on bottom middle of fan and glue to fix (*sketch d*). Let dry.
- To fix fan to bamboo, wrap string around cardboard strips and bamboo (*sketch e*). Tie ends.
- Spread out folds of the fan (*sketch f*). Wave to create a cool breeze.

Life in Bible Times

What do you like to do to cool off on a hot day? In Bible times, there was no air conditioning. Fans made from ostrich feathers or palm fronds were used to keep air circulating and create cool breezes. On a warm day, a king might instruct a servant to fan him. If the servant obeyed willingly, he was considered wise.

A king delights in a wise servant... Proverbs 14:35

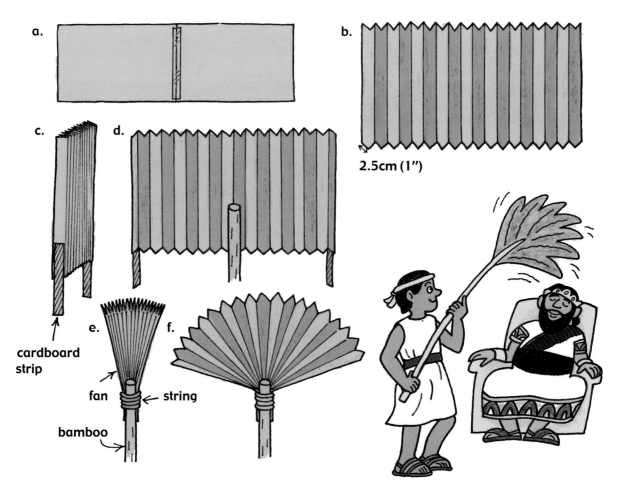

a.

b.

2.5cm (1")

c.

d.

cardboard strip

e.

fan ← string

bamboo

f.

Torch

Ages 4 – 9

Materials

- Bamboo (from craft shop) or 2.5cm (1 inch) dowel
- Saw
- Pencils
- Tape measure
- Scissors
- Brown wrapping paper
- Large plastic or paper cups
- Transparent tape
- PVA glue
- Hot glue gun
- Glue sticks
- Cardboard
- Red, yellow and orange crêpe-paper streamers

Preparation by grown-up

- Saw bamboo or dowel into 90cm (1 yard) lengths – one for each child.

- Trace around bottom of cup onto cardboard and cut out circle – one for each child.
- Glue a cardboard circle to one end of each bamboo or dowel length (*sketch a*). Let it dry. Cut the streamers into 1.8m (2 yard) lengths.
- From brown paper, cut rectangles to be wrapped around plastic cups (*sketch b*) – one for each child.

Method

- Wrap brown paper rectangle around cup and tape to secure (*sketch b*).
- Cut streamers at an angle into various lengths which are slightly taller than the cup (*sketch c*).
- Squeeze a line of glue along bottom of streamers.
- Placing longer streamers in the centre and shorter streamers around the edge, glue inside cup for "flames" (*sketch d*).
- Teachers use hot glue gun to glue bottom of cup to cardboard circle on the end of bamboo (*sketch d*). Let dry.

Life in Bible Times

When you go out on a dark night, how do you see where you're going? In Bible times, a person walking at night sometimes carried a torch. The night that Jesus was arrested, he prayed in the Garden of Gethsemane. Judas led soldiers into the garden. The soldiers carried torches as they came to arrest Jesus.

So Judas came to the grove, guiding a detachment of soldiers and some officials from the chief priests and Pharisees. They were carrying torches, lanterns and weapons.
John 18:3

a.

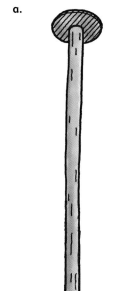

b.

c.

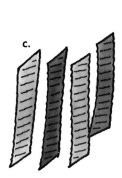

d.

Chains

Materials

- Scissors
- Craft knife
- Staplers and staples
- Ruler
- Silver Paint
- Wool
- Hole punch

For each child

- Two cardboard tubes

Preparation by grown-up

- Use craft knife or miniature saw to cut tubes into 2.5cm (1 inch) hoops (*sketch a*).
- Paint hoops.

Method

- Cut an opening in each hoop (*sketch b*).
- With the exception of two, link hoops together and staple to form a chain (*sketch c*).
- Punch two holes in each end hoop (*sketch d*).
- Punch two holes in each of the two remaining hoops.
- Use wool to link remaining hoops to chain (*sketch d*).
- Wear chains by placing an end hoop on each wrist.

Life in Bible Times

After Jesus went to heaven, his disciples went to many cities telling people the good news about Jesus. The leaders in some cities didn't want the disciples to talk about Jesus. They ordered the disciples to be put in jail with chains on their hands and feet.

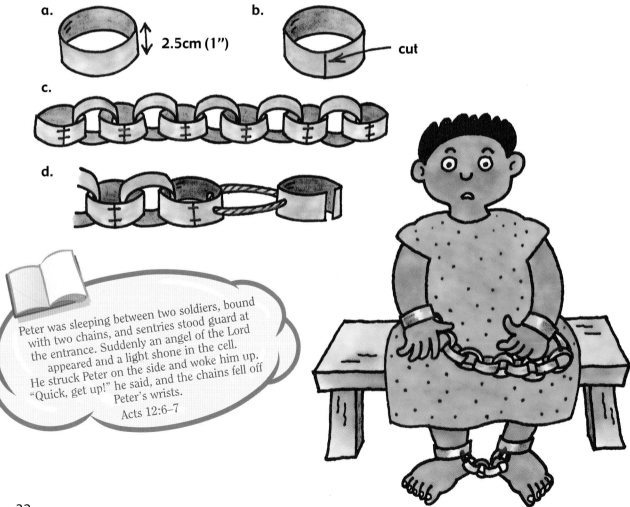

a.

2.5cm (1")

b.

cut

c.

d.

Peter was sleeping between two soldiers, bound with two chains, and sentries stood guard at the entrance. Suddenly an angel of the Lord appeared and a light shone in the cell. He struck Peter on the side and woke him up. "Quick, get up!" he said, and the chains fell off Peter's wrists.
Acts 12:6–7

Copyright © 2006 Lion Hudson plc/Tim Dowley and
Peter Wyart trading as Three's Company

Published in 2006 by Candle Books
(a publishing imprint of Lion Hudson plc).

Distributed in the UK by Marston Book Services Ltd,
PO Box 269, Abingdon, Oxon OX14 4YN

Distributed in the USA by Kregel Publications,
Grand Rapids, Michigan 49501

UK   ISBN-13: 978-1-85985-622-2
     ISBN-10: 1-85985-622-5

USA ISBN-13: 978-0-8254-7309-8
     ISBN-10: 0-8254-7309-8

Contents Copyright © 1993 Gospel Light, Ventura,
California 93006.

Scripture quotations taken from the *Holy Bible, New
International Version,* copyright © 1973, 1978, 1984
International Bible Society. Used by permission of
Zondervan and Hodder & Stoughton Limited.

Worldwide co-edition produced by
Lion Hudson plc,
Mayfield House, 256 Banbury Road,
Oxford OX2 7DH, England.
Telephone: +44 (0) 1865 302750.
Fax: +44 (0) 1865 302757.
Email: coed@lionhudson.com.
www.lionhudson.com

Printed in Singapore

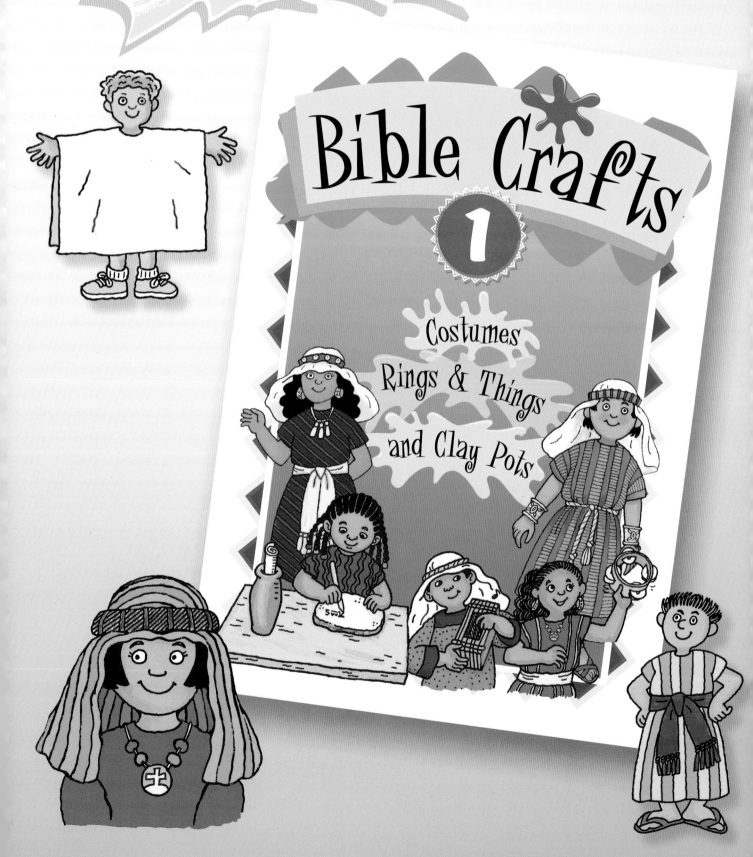

ALSO AVAILABLE

Bible Crafts
1

Costumes
Rings & Things
and Clay Pots